Green Is Like a Meadow of Grass;

AN ANTHOLOGY OF CHILDREN'S PLEASURE IN POETRY,

selected by Nancy Larrick

drawings by Kelly Oechsli

Pub. Co.

GARRARD PUBLISHING COMPANY
CHAMPAIGN, ILLINOIS

Green Is Like a Meadow of Grass has grown out of the enthusiastic experimentation of teachers who participated in the 1967 Lehigh University Workshop in Poetry for Children and of their pupils who responded with the poetic pictures which make up this anthology. The teachers:

Helena Bowman, Bunnell School, East Stroudsburg, Pa.

Irmgard Cistone, Brensinger Elementary School, Phillipsburg, N. J.

Cynthia Gordon, Palmer Elementary School, Easton, Pa.

Karen Hein, Doyle Elementary School, Doylestown, Pa.

Lynn Lynch, Wolf Elementary School, Hellertown, Pa.

Lucille Y. Stewart, Governor Wolf Elementary School, Bethlehem, Pa.

Joann Mahoney, Washington Elementary School, Bethlehem, Pa.

Kathleen Libricz, Viola Long, and Jane Thomas, Miller Heights Elementary School, Bethlehem, Pa.

Judith Fouchaux, Barbara Landis, Audrey McGinn, and Kay Winters, Lehigh Laboratory School, Bethlehem, Pa.

Library of Congress Catalog Card Number: 68-16159

Green Is Like a Meadow of Grass

To many people, green is green and nothing more. But to someone who sees more than the camera sees, green is like a gumdrop or a four-leaf clover. Green is things growing, like a meadow of grass. Or green is coolness and contentment.

The person who sees with his imagination finds a dinosaur in the clouds or a dancer in a swaying tree. If he uses paint and brush to record his picture, he is using the tools of an artist. If he creates his picture with words, he is following the way of the poet.

Children seem to have a flair for creating poetic pictures with words. One will pick up a sea shell and say, "Why, it's a fairy's fan!" Another, watching autumn leaves falling to the wet sidewalk, may say, "They shine like copper pennies."

Like gifted poets, children have a way of looking at the world around them and then letting their imagination take over. Often their word pictures have the ring of real poetry.

During the spring of 1967, several hundred boys and girls in the area of Bethlehem, Pennsylvania, had an opportunity to listen to poetry and read or recite it almost every day. They began to see poetic pictures in the spring snow that covered their world for a few days and the mud puddles that followed. Soon they were creating their own poetic images and snatches of song. From these, seventy-four have been selected for *Green Is Like a Meadow of Grass,* an anthology of children's pleasure in poetry.

—*Nancy Larrick*

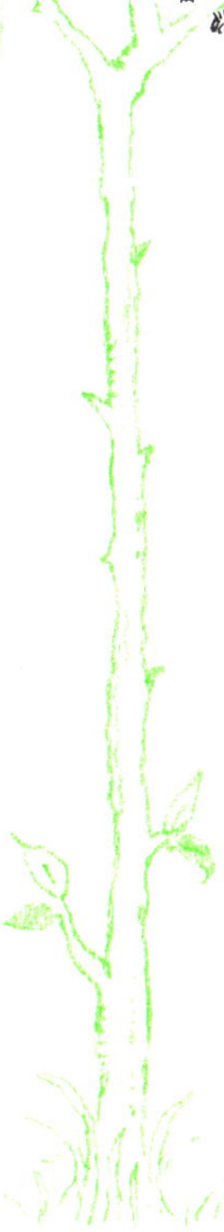

CONTENTS

It's Snowing . . . It's Blowing . . .

It's snowing
It's blowing
What a beautiful sight
Outside our window
    clear and bright.
It's slishy
It's sloshy
It's splishy
    and sploshy.

—Patricia Romanick, age 8

The snow, the snow
Do you fall
Down down
From the sky?
Do you float
Down?
Do you fall on trees
And on houses
And on schools?
Of course you do.

—Raymond Herman, age 8

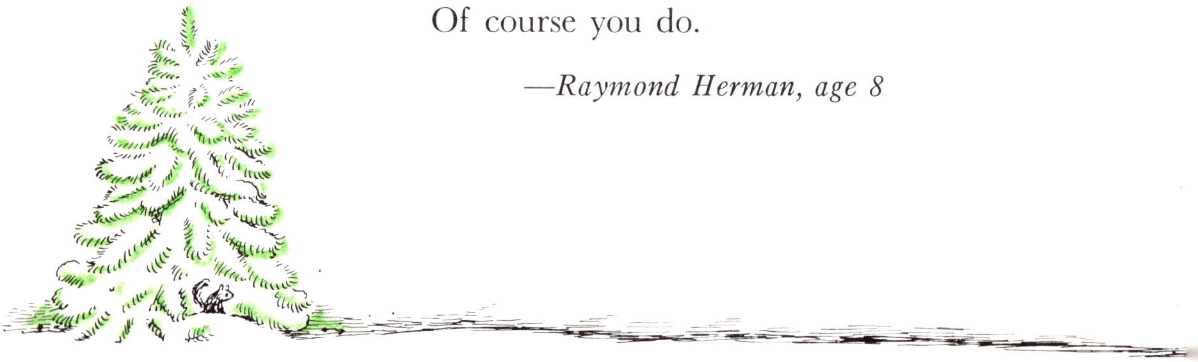

When it snows,
All the trees and bushes
Put on their lovely white nightgowns.
And go to sleep.
Then snow covers the trees
And all the bushes
With a white blanket.

—*Glen Jacoby, age 7*

Spring Is a Happy Time

SPRING

Spring is a happy time.
a merry time, a good time.
We plant trees.
We plant flowers.
We plant, we plant, we plant
in spring.

—Joseph Subits, age 7

The March wind blows my kite
up into the air above the clouds
and blows me home.

—Judy Parr, age 7

Daisy

A daisy is like a ballerina
The petals go up and down.
When the daisy closes,
The ballerina dies in the ground.

—Lorraine Reiss, age 9

Daffodils

Daffodils are pieces of the sun
That have fallen to the ground.

—Kyle Diane Sutton, age 9

BLUEBELLS

When you hold bluebells upside down,
They look like midget chandeliers.
The little blue bells are candles.

—Joe Szabo, age 8

Grass is greener in the spring
It stands up nice and straight
Like tin soldiers at attention.

—Jimmy Van Billiard, age 8

The Pine Trees

They look like giant hair brushes
With pine cones as snarls to be brushed out.

—*Mary Angela Caroprese, age 10*

THE TREE

I am green and black
I shelter animals from rain, lightning and
    thunder.
I reach out my arms
    to protect small animals from harm.

—Joseph Rose, age 12

The Wind

The wind is like a soothing fan
    that blows the curtains and cools me
    on a hot summer's night.
It carries wonderful dreams
To keep me company while I sleep.

—Cindy Wilson, age 11

One Morning There Was Fog

The White Monster

One morning when I got up
there was fog.
It looked like a monster
eating up buildings and houses
and cars and trees and roads.
When I walked down the street
the white monster ate me up.

—Teresa Trubilla, age 7

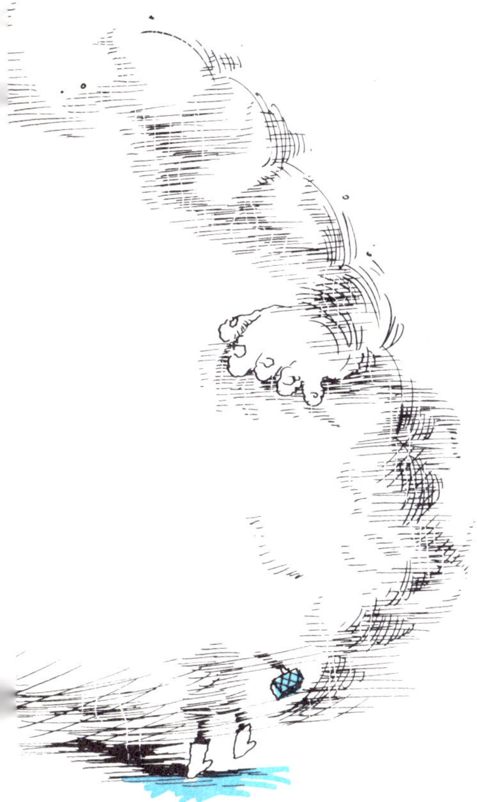

Fog

Fog, we cannot see through you.
You are like a pillow.
You are like feathers.
You are white like snow.
You are a cloud.

—Nancy Lou Nagy, age 7

I wonder if my jack knife
Slipped out of my pocket
And cut holes in the clouds.

—Joseph Ricci, age 8

Rain

What is that little pitter-patter
    on my window?
Could it be a little elf
    playing a trick on me?

—Joan Fegley, age 10

When the rain beats on the sidewalk
It seems like our cat
Walking over the bed.

—Patricia Romanick, age 8

The Story of Rain

I like pearls and
I like raindrops that fall on my roof.
I like when the rain hits other rain
it makes crowns pop up.
It blooms the flowers and it hits my umbrella.
The rain makes a sound that makes me dance.
When the flowers bloom
I will give a flower to my teacher
And the flower pops out of the ground
like me.

—Latressa Atwood, age 8

Rain on the Housetops . . .
Rain on the Trees

Rain taps on your windows,
Giants running on the clouds
Flashing their flashlights.

Drip drop on the roof
Like little rocks thrown up there.

Rain in the street
Like a lake for ants.

Rain on the grass
Like a machine gun.

Thunder is a running horse.
Thunder is giants bowling.

When it lightens
A giant gets a strike.

Rain on the windows
Like silver stones,
Like bullets
Heading toward your windshield,
Like silver dots on the glass,
Like people walking tippytoe
On your car roof.

When rain drops on flowers
It makes a little noise
Like a ladybug walking on grass.

—*First Graders, Cynthia Gordon, Teacher*
Palmer Elementary School, Easton, Pa.

Tippity-tap
The rain is falling
Falling on my bumbershoot.
It taps like fingers snapping.

—Katy Fouchaux, age 6

April Showers

I like it when it rains in April.
Then I can get a shower under trees
Or wiggle my toes in the mud
When I go barefoot.

—Teresa Trubilla, age 7

The rain
makes little stars
when it comes down in puddles.

—Judy Parr, age 7

The Puddle

Alone in the dark and light
Sits the puddle full of mud
The dirtiest piece of water
And the enemy
Of all little children's mothers.

—Mary Angela Caroprese, age 10

The rain falls like pussywillows
They fall dancing.

—Iris Luciano, age 8

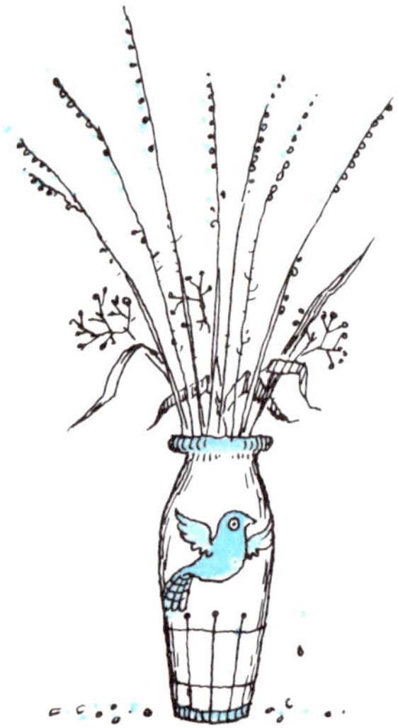

PUDDLES

Muddy, gooey mud puddles,
They come on every rainy day,
And when I looked in one
I saw a muddy face.
It looked like me
            charcoal black.

—Debbie Ricker, age 10

Green Is Like a Meadow of Grass

After reading *Hailstones and Halibut Bones* by Mary O'Neill

Green is like a meadow of grass
Banana peels that are not ripe
And broccoli.

—*Beth Smith, age 8*

Green is in summertime trees,
Green is in a sweet mint breeze.

—*Mary Sunderland, age 8*

What is white?
A swan is white
I feel white when I look at it.
The clouds are white
I feel white when I look at them.

What is white?
A lamb is white
It is so soft
I feel white when I touch it.

—Robin Mudri, age 7

What is gold?
Gold is a golden ring
Sitting on a pillow.
Gold is like a golden dress
Maybe Miss Mahoney has.

—William Goosley, age 8

Gray is a feeling
like forgetting your lunch.

—Cindy Peifly, age 8

Blue is like the wind staggering
Through the sky.
Blue is like the bluebirds
Making nests in trees.

—Susan Hawes, age 8

Yellow is tons of corn
Shovel yellow on the wagon,
Shovel yellow off a wagon.
Yellow gives you pain in the muscles.
Yellow, goodbye.

—William Newhard, age 10

Brown is sad.
It makes me think of muddy shoes
Just waiting to be cleaned.

—Robert Kerecz, age 8

Brown

I like brown
 because paper bags
  are brown
 And Negroes
  are brown
  sitting in the sun.
I like brown
 because roots are brown.

—Chris Pivnichny, age 7

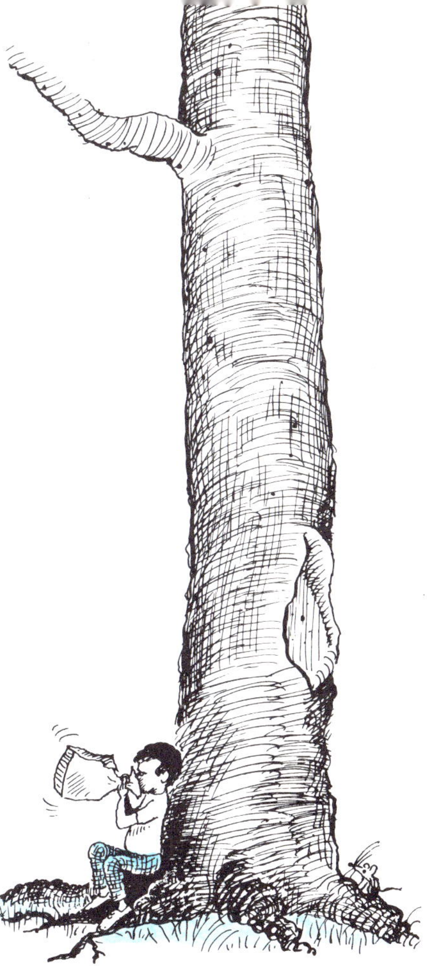

Black Black

I think of boats
and roads,
and telephone wires
and oil and top hats
and lead
and my dog is black.

—Raymond Herman, age 8

I Have a Little Sea Shell

I have a little sea shell.
It feels very soft.
Inside my sea shell you can hear a little
Sh-sh-sh shp
Which is the sea.

—Elaine Kunkle, age 7

The sea shell is singing to me
And I sing back to the sea shell.

—Debra Johnson, age 8

I like the sound of a sea shell,
It sounds like a night
When it gales and storms,
When a ship's at sea
Blowing its fog horn.

—Dave Hobbs, age 8

My shell is like a wing,
White and green and smooth;
Like spring
But with no snow.

—Susan Dardes, age 7

A turkey's tail spread out
Brown and white
The turkey lives on a water farm
With a starfish for a farmer.

—Joseph Amoroso, age 7

Little shell, with colors so gay and pretty,
You look like a butterfly
Resting your wings along the shore.

—Rosemary Van Why, age 8

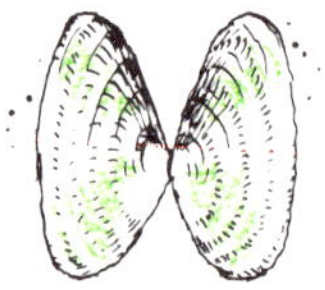

It looks like a fan
With all different colors
Opened wide on the beach.

—Ricky Frankenfield, age 8

When a wave comes by
The shell comes closer to the beach
Like a little motor boat.

—Brent Curtis, age 8

The sea shell has a shiny clean scrubbed face
With a funny nose.

—Richard Kiak, age 9

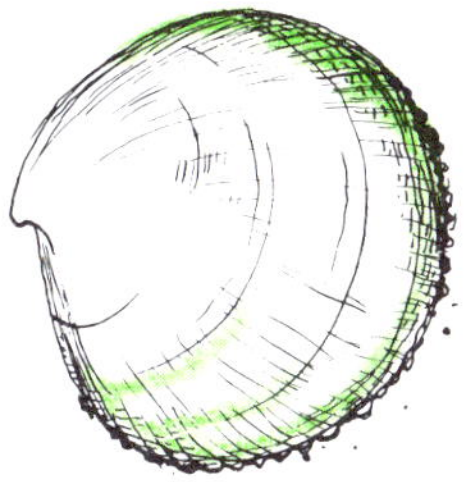

Underneath
The sea sings
And on top
The waves are as big as hills.

—Tommy Folk, age 7

The sea is full of clams
Doing a dance
With the tide.

—Ingo Georgoff, age 7

As the tide goes out
It may leave little pools.
Sea creatures gather there.
When you wiggle your feet in the pools
They may tickle your toes.

—James Fischer, age 9

A water sprite wears slipper shells
On her feet.

—*Keith Green, age 9*

Lacy sea shell
So perfect and white,
Did a fairy leave behind
Her pink frill for your lining?

—*Debra Seip, age 9*

SEA SHELLS

One by one the fairies
walk in a little sea shell.
They go into the little halls,
the halls of color.
They walk onto tippety top
and then they start to sing.

—William Goosley, age 8

I Like Fairies

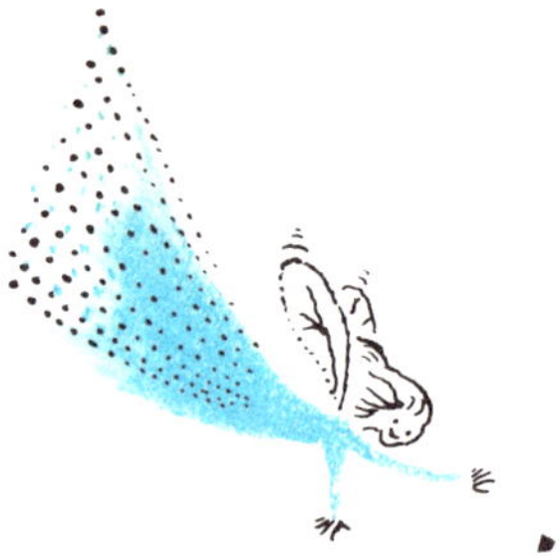

I like fairies that float on the clouds
and fly down my chimney.

—Katy Fouchaux, age 6

A fairy is like a swan
flying through the sky
with her wings blowing
in back of her like the wind,
blowing right on top of me.

—Ruth Isaac, age 7

Fairies

Fairies live in another world,
A world of mystery.
Fairyland is where children go
To take their troubles.

—Donald Koehler, age 12

I wish I was lucky.
I wish I had a lamp
That when I say I love fairies,
I'd get a play one.
And I wish everything sparkled.

—Latressa Atwood, age 8

I Like to Play with the Moon

I like to play with the moon.
Sometimes we play soccer
I hit the moon 40 feet up.

—Fernando Gonzalez, age 8

I like to go to the moon
to play baseball
with the world.
I'll take a stick
in a space capsule for a bat.

—George Gotthardt, age 9

I know a star that goes around in circles.
When I go to bed every night
I see my friend watching me.

—Perry Nardella, age 6

Pancakes

Pancakes are like flying saucers
In the morning they come down at me
So I can eat them.
I attack them with cinnamon
And pancake syrup.

—Glen Jacoby, age 7

If I were a top
I would spin and spin
till I dropped down dizzy.

—Erig E. Frey, age 8

INDIANS

Feathers for a hat—
War paint for the skin,
Arrows for a war,
White men to battle.

—William Newhard, age 10

The Stinky City

The stinky city
Rolls by my nose.
It sprouts and yells
Those stinky smells.
Inside my car
It's nice and warm.
The city is yellow
With the sun.

—Ruth Isaac, age 7

Roof Tops

Roof tops are pencil points.
Roof tops are arrow tips.
Roof tops are chalk boards,
And they all please me.

—Kirk Gorkos, age 9

Work for Yobo

Street sweeping is part of this borough, Man's life.
A swish of vibrating wet sleaky water
Then people are mad
Because of their dirty laundry.
Dust flying all over
Is not the purpose of men we know.
I am sorry, Man.
So back in the fluffy soft seat
And away I go.

—*John Bautista, age 9*

Our Prayers from the Ark

After reading *Prayers from the Ark*
by Carmen Bernos de Gasztold

The Snake

I hiss while I am hunting down my prey.
Everyone runs any old way.
Lord! perhaps you can make them understand
I'm not made to sing like a bird.

—Michael Kerecz, age 10

The Mouse

Well, God . . . You see I want to be
Out in the open
With all the other animals
Eating out of big bowls.
I don't want to be a gray thing
With blobs
That cats run after
Every day.
Up in your world . . .
Will you fly me there?

—Ruth Isaac, age 7

THE WORM

Because I am a worm
I am food for the birds,
And used as bait for fish.
Dear God!
Could you find a better use for me?

—*Celeste Applegate, age 11*

THE GIRAFFE

Oh, Lord, please keep that elephant
Off my foot.
My foot is delicate
And it hurts. *Amen*

—*Ingo Georgoff, age 7*

THE ANT

Dear God!
I have six legs to walk from place to place,
Other creatures do not have that many.
But did you have to make my legs so much shorter?
The bigger ones can destroy me with just one of theirs.

—*Joseph Kransnai, age 12*

THE MOUSE

I would like to know why all the cats chase me.
And why people set a trap to catch me.
I want to thank you, Lord,
for making me smart enough
to miss some of the traps
so I can live a little while longer.

—Robert Vargo, age 13

The Bee

Everyone is always trying to kill me
Or squirt me with DDT.
Dear God! Why did you give me a stinger?
I can't help it, but when I get angry,
I'm forced to use it.

—Renée Weiss, age 10

A Spider

Dear God
I weave all day
I get so tired
Why do you let people hit me?

—Emily Schramm, age 8

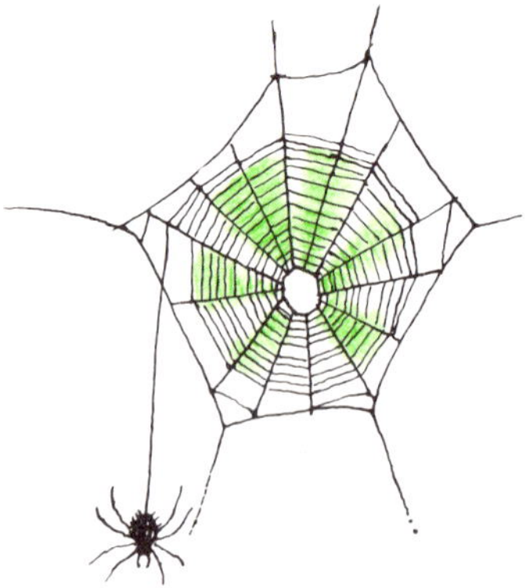

A Fly

This is the small winged buzzer speaking.
I wish I could go underground
And get away from that cursed spider
And people with their swatters.

—Gavin Steif, age 8

Frogs

Lord,
People say we are slippery and slimy,
Gooey and grimy.
That slimy old stuff is just water and greens.
Why do they treat us as if we were mud?

—Barbara Bauder, age 11

A kitten is a little thing
That's huggable.
The sound it makes
When you are lonely
Fills your heart.

—Judy Parr, age 7

BY WAY OF EXPLANATION

During the spring of 1967, the third Workshop in Poetry for Children was held at Lehigh University as a regular graduate course in the School of Education. Twenty-two teachers met for three hours each Wednesday afternoon to read poetry and experiment with the most effective ways of introducing children and poetry. Their classrooms became laboratories, where close to 500 elementary school children listened to poetry and read, recited or sang it nearly every day.

The sound of poetry won almost every listener from the beginning, particularly when children were given the opportunity to participate. The youngest sang "Twinkle, Twinkle, Little Star" and "Mary Had a Little Lamb." First grade boys would chant in unison the numbers in "One, two, buckle my shoe" and girls would recite the rest of each line. Children of all ages sang and skipped to "Skip to My Lou," inventing new stanzas as they went.

Such folk songs as "Fly Through My Window" and "Bought Me a Cat" gave them a chance to sing in large or small groups and to improvise. Even those children who had hitherto remained silent were drawn into the singing or impromptu group reading.

While the sounds of poetry and songs were winning more and more participants, we encouraged children to note fresh and colorful word pictures in their everyday language. The names of such birds as the *cuckoo, whippoorwill* and *bobwhite* suggested other words which imitate sound: *crash, tinkle, rip, squeak,* for example. Christina Rossetti's poem, "What Is Pink?", launched them into noting and then recording or dictating their own explanation of various colors. This led to our reading Mary O'Neill's wonderful collection of color poems, *Hailstones and Halibut Bones.* From this came many color poems by the children. For weeks Mary O'Neill was their favorite poet.

It became clear that children respond more readily to poetry when they have had a hand in creating poetry of their own, either orally or on paper. As a beginning, we encouraged children to observe and then let their imagination take over. When rain beat on the schoolroom window, a teacher would ask her children to look and listen and then tell what this suggested. From the playground, they would look at the clouds and try to see new pictures and then write about them.

Once we experimented with sea shells, spreading them out on a table and asking the students to find names for the shells that would suggest what the shell looked like or how it was made. Then the children recorded their ideas, expanding them as they wrote.

When we read Carmen Bernos de Gatztold's *Prayers from the Ark,* the children quickly put themselves in the place of each animal and felt its plaintive plea. Soon many were writing their own petitions. Five- and six-year-olds dictated theirs.

At no time did we suggest the use of rhyme. In fact, we discouraged attempts at rhyming lines because at this stage rhyme seems to force a child into goose-step thinking.

As the children wrote their own poetic images and listened to the rhythmic lines of published poetry, they became more sensitive to fresh and original ideas in both poetry and prose. Their pleasure in reading and writing expanded remarkably.

During the fifteen weeks of the workshop, thousands of poetic images were recorded by the children. Some were only a line or two. Others were longer. But the youngsters soon realized that it is not length that makes a poem good. And it is not rhyme, for a poem does not have to rhyme. But it does have to spring from imagination expressing some new idea, painting a unique picture, stirring the reader to think and feel as he has never done before. From these children's pleasure in poetry, comes *Green Is Like a Meadow of Grass.*

—Nancy Larrick

Index of Authors